Snake's

The Characters

 Narrator

 Rabbit

 Snake

 Coyote

Narrator: One day, a big rock fell on Snake.

 Snake: Help! Help!

 Rabbit: Maybe Snake is trying to trick me, or maybe he really needs help.

Narrator: Rabbit was afraid of Snake, but he wanted to help.

 Rabbit: Maybe I can push the rock off your back.

 Snake: Push it off, and I will give you a reward.

4

Narrator: Rabbit pushed and pushed. He pushed the rock off Snake.

 Snake: Can you guess what your reward will be?

 Rabbit: No. What?

Snake: I am going
to eat you.
That is your reward.

 Rabbit: That is
not fair. I helped you.
I pushed the rock
off your back.

 Snake: I needed
help then, but now
I do not need help.
So I will eat you.

Rabbit: No! No! That is not fair!

 Snake: Yes! Yes! That is fair!

 Narrator: Along came Coyote.

Rabbit: I helped
Snake, Coyote.
I pushed the rock
off his back.
Now he is going
to eat me.
That is not fair.

 Snake: Yes, it is fair.
I needed help then.
I do not need
help now.

13

Coyote: I need to see how things were. Let me push the rock back on you, Snake.

 Snake: Very well. Take a look, Coyote. Now get this rock off me.

Coyote: Now I see. Snake, it is fair for you to have the rock as your reward.

 Rabbit: Ha-ha-ha!

 Coyote: Ha-ha-ha!